CUS

Queen Elizabeth I

Liz Gogerly

First published in 2007 by Wayland
Copyright © Wayland 2007

Wayland
338 Euston Road
London NW1 3BH

Wayland Australia
Level 17/207 Kent Street
Sydney, NSW 2000

Editor: Victoria Brooker
Designer: Jane Stanley

Gogerly, Liz
    Who was Elizabeth I?
    1. Elizabeth, I, Queen of England, 1533-1603 - Juvenile
    literature 2. Great Britain - Kings and rulers - Biography
    - Juvenile literature 3. Great Britain - History -
    Elizabeth I, 1558-1603 - Juvenile literature
    I. Title
    942'.055'092
ISBN 978 0 7502 5192 1
Printed in China
Wayland is a division of Hachette Children's Books.

For permission to reproduce the following pictures, the author and publisher would like to
thank: British Library (Add.35324)/Heritage-Images: 21; Burghley House Collection,
Lincolnshire, UK/Bridgeman Art Library, London: 6; ©Eric Crichton/Corbis: 7; ©Gillian
Darley, Edifice/Corbis: 16; Getty Images (Hulton Archive): 14; Helmingham Hall, Suffolk,
UK/Mark Fiennes/Bridgeman Art Library: 9; Loseley Park: 17; Loseley Park, Guildford,
Surrey, UK/Mark Fiennes/Bridgeman Art Library, London: 8; National Museum and
Gallery of Wales, Cardiff, UK/Bridgeman Art Library, London: 10; National Portrait
Gallery, London/Bridgeman Art Library, London: 12; Print Collector/Heritage-Images: 4,
Cover; Walter Rawlings/Robert Harding World Imagery/Corbis: 11; St Faith's Church,
Gaywood, Norfolk, UK/Bridgeman Art Library, London: 19; Stapleton Collection/
Bridgeman Art Library, London: 5; Victoria & Albert Museum, London/Bridgeman Art
Library, London: 18; Walker Art Gallery, National Museums Liverpool/Bridgeman Art
Library, London: 15; Woburn Abbey, Bedfordshire, UK/Bridgeman Art Library, London: 1,
20; Yale Center for British Art, Paul Mellon Collection, USA/Bridgeman Art Library: 13

The website addresses (URLs) included in this book were valid at the time of going to
press. However, because of the nature of the Internet, it is possible that some addresses
may have changed, or sites may have changed or closed down since publication. While
the author and Publisher regret any inconvenience this may cause the readers, no
responsibility for any such changes can be accepted by either the author or the Publisher.

Contents

Words in **bold** can be found in the glossary.

Who was Queen Elizabeth I?

Elizabeth I was Queen of England from 1558 to 1603. Her **reign** lasted 45 years. She was well loved by her people. They often called her Good Queen Bess. We call the time she reigned the Elizabethan age.

All through her reign Elizabeth had her portrait painted. This picture was copied and sent all round the country.

Elizabeth was the last Tudor **monarch**. The Tudors were a family of kings and queens. Elizabeth's grandfather, Henry VII, was the first Tudor king.

Elizabeth wanted to be seen by her people. On special occasions she sat in an open carrier called a litter.

Birth of a princess

Elizabeth was born on 7 September 1533 at Greenwich Palace, London. Her parents were King Henry VIII of England and his second wife Anne Boleyn.

A portrait of King Henry VIII. Elizabeth had her father's red hair and her mother's brown eyes.

In Tudor times, people thought kings made better rulers than queens. Henry wanted a son to be **heir** to the throne. He was so disappointed that he had a girl that he did not go to Elizabeth's **christening**.

Places to Visit

Hatfield House, in Hertfordshire, the place where Elizabeth lived as a girl. She did not see her parents very often. Nannies and governesses looked after the young princess.

Elizabeth loved the gardens and woods at Hatfield House where she grew up.

A clever young lady

Henry fell out of love with Anne Boleyn. In 1536 he had Anne Boleyn **beheaded**. Elizabeth was just two years old. The same year Henry married Jane Seymour. They had a boy called Edward.

This portrait is of Edward when he was about 11 years old.

Elizabeth was a clever girl. Her teachers taught her languages and history. She shared her lessons with her half-brother Edward. They cared for each other very much.

Places to Visit

Hampton Court Palace on the Thames. Elizabeth often stayed at this royal palace when she was a girl.

Elizabeth enjoyed playing musical instruments and dancing. She played a stringed instrument called a lute.

Princess in prison

Henry VIII died in 1547 and Edward was **crowned** king. Sadly, King Edward VI died when he was sixteen. His half-sister Mary took the throne. Queen Mary was not popular. Some people **plotted** to make Elizabeth queen instead.

A portrait of Henry VIII with Edward, Jane Seymour, Mary and Elizabeth.

In 1554 Elizabeth was arrested and locked up in the Tower of London. Elizabeth had done nothing wrong. After two months Mary released her. Queen Mary died in 1558 and Elizabeth became the new queen of England.

Places to Visit

The Tower of London. Henry VII built rooms for the royal family there during his **reign**. Later, when Henry VIII was king, prisoners were kept in the Tower.

Today the Tower of London is no longer used as a prison. It is where the **Crown Jewels** are kept.

Queen of Hearts

Elizabeth was **crowned** at Westminster Abbey in January 1559. As she paraded through the streets she took time to speak to, and shake hands with, ordinary people. They loved their new queen.

Elizabeth's coronation painting. The night before the big day she told her people: 'I will be as good unto ye as ever a Queen was unto her people.'

In Tudor times **monarchs** were expected to get married. Many kings asked Elizabeth to be their wife. In the end she did not marry. She said that the Kingdom of England was her husband.

Elizabeth loved a man called Robert Dudley. He was already married but they stayed close friends until his death in 1588.

A strong leader

Elizabeth wanted to prove that a woman could be a strong leader. Each day she made decisions about how the country was run. In those days **Parliament** did not have the power it has today. The Queen decided when Parliament would meet. She also passed new laws.

Elizabeth often called Parliament just because she needed money.

In 1559 Elizabeth called Parliament. She wanted to make religious changes. The Church of England was reformed. Elizabeth was made **Supreme Governor of the Church**. This helped to make the country more peaceful.

Elizabeth enjoyed receiving visitors from abroad. The queen always wore her jewels and finest clothes to impress them.

Entertaining the Queen

Elizabeth I enjoyed drama, music, poetry and art. The playwright William Shakespeare wrote plays for her. Edmund Spenser presented her with the poem *The Faerie Queen*. Elizabeth arranged free concerts at the Royal Exchange in London for the poor.

The new Globe theatre in London. It is built like the Globe theatre of Elizabeth's day.

Each year the Queen went on a tour of the great country houses of the day. Banquets and tournaments were all laid on for her pleasure. Some people even created new rooms or gardens for the Queen's visit.

Places to Visit

Shakespeare's Globe Theatre in London. Elizabeth enjoyed visiting the original theatre to see the plays of William Shakespeare.

This bedroom at Loseley Hall in Surrey was once used by Elizabeth I.

Elizabeth at war

Many people **plotted** against
Elizabeth I. Elizabeth's cousin,
Mary Queen of Scots, was found
guilty of plotting against the
Queen. She was **beheaded** in 1587.
This made Elizabeth many enemies.

A portrait of Mary
Queen of Scots.
Many people thought
Elizabeth was jealous
of Mary's beauty.

In 1588 King Philip II launched a fleet of ships to invade England. The Spanish fleet was called the Armada. The English Navy eventually beat the Spanish. Elizabeth proved she was a strong leader.

IT'S TRUE!

Sir Francis Drake was the first Englishman to sail around the world. During his voyages he stole treasure from the Spanish. He shared everything with the Queen.

Elizabeth visited her troops at Tilbury. She gave a famous speech. It gave the men courage and helped them to beat the Spanish Armada.

The final years

As she grew older Elizabeth enjoyed the company of a young man called Robert Devereux, Earl of Essex. He **plotted** against her and was **executed** in 1601. Meanwhile, rising costs caused riots in parts of England. Elizabeth became sad and unwell.

A portrait of the queen painted to celebrate the victory over Spain. Her clothes, jewellery and make-up make her look rich and powerful.

In 1603, after months of ill health, Elizabeth died. She was sixty-nine. In her last hours she chose James VI of Scotland to be king. He became James I of England. Elizabeth was buried at Westminster Abbey.

Places to Visit

Elizabeth's tomb is in the Henry VII Chapel at Westminster Abbey in London. Elizabeth was also **crowned** here in 1559.

Elizabeth's funeral **procession**. The streets of London were filled with people crying.

Timeline

September 1533	Elizabeth born at Greenwich Palace, London
May 1536	Elizabeth's mother, Anne Boleyn, beheaded
October 1537	Elizabeth's brother Edward VI born Elizabeth's step-mother, Jane Seymour, dies
January 1547	Elizabeth's father, Henry VIII, dies Edward VI becomes king of England
July 1553	Edward VI dies Mary I becomes queen of England
1554	Elizabeth imprisoned in the Tower of London
November 1558	Mary I dies Elizabeth I becomes queen of England
January 1559	Elizabeth crowned at Westminster Abbey, London
1568	Mary Queen of Scots is imprisoned
1577-1580	Sir Francis Drake sails around the world in his ship *The Golden Hind*
1586	Mary Queen of Scots found guilty of plotting against the Queen
February 1587	Mary Queen of Scots beheaded
1588	King Philip II attempts to invade England
March 1603	Queen Elizabeth I dies

Glossary

beheaded to have the head cut off

christening a Christian ceremony in which a person is accepted into the Christian Church

crowned to crown somebody is to give them the royal crown and make them king or queen of a country

Crown Jewels the crowns, swords, rings and other jewels that are used and worn by the English monarch during the coronation ceremony or other important occasions

executed to execute a person is to kill somebody as a punishment for a crime

guilty if you are guilty, you have committed a crime or done something wrong

heir the heir to the throne becomes the next monarch of a country

monarch the ruler of a country, such as a king or queen

Parliament a group of people who have been elected to pass the laws of a country

plotted to make a secret plan

procession a number of people and carriages that travel along a planned route as part of a public festival or occasion

reign to rule as a king or queen or the time that a king or queen stays on the throne

Supreme Governor of the Church the title held by the monarch of Great Britain which means they are head of the Church of England

Further information

Books

Elizabeth I (Beginners) by S. R Turnbull (Usborne, 2004)

Queen Elizabeth I: British History Makers by Leon Ashworth (Evans Brother, 2002)

Websites

http://www.historyonthenet.com/Lessons/elizabeth1/who_was_elizabeth_i.htm

An on-line lesson which tells the story of Elizabeth's life.

http://www.toweroflondontour.com/kids/

A friendly raven is your tour guide of the Tower of London in England. This site is great fun with music, games and colourful pictures.

Index